Things To Shout Out Loud At Parties

Markus Almond

Copyright © 2014 by Markus Almond. All Rights Reserved.
Published by Brooklyn To Mars Books

CONTENTS

Introduction	5
Part One	7
Part Two	39
Part Three	101
Part Four	151
Conclusion	199

INTRODUCTION

Hello. I am Markus Almond and this is an introduction.

I run a little magazine called Brooklyn To Mars. Lately, I've been getting emails from people saying they've been reading my stuff out loud with their friends. This made me smile because I used to do the same thing with my roommates when we had a poetry book laying around.

My friends and I used to live in this giant, old church. None of us were religious. We just did volunteer work in exchange for a place to live. Some of us were artists or musicians or working on various projects. But mostly, we just liked to hang out. The congregation never knew that on the weekends, we would throw massive parties with kegs and DJs after the sun went down. Sometimes it got a little out of control. But on normal nights, when it was calm and we had a few friends over, one of my roommates would take out a poetry book and we'd read it around the fireplace. We'd pass around a bottle and all take turns reading a page or two out loud.

Things To Shout Out Loud At Parties is a collection of paraprose written in the spirit of those nights. There are tales of love and redemption, glimpses of adventure and sex and even a few strange tales about the things that can sometimes destroy us.

But no matter how far we fall, I find that we can usually pull ourselves through with the right friends around.

I'd like to dedicate this book to those people that were there with me during those shout-out-loud nights. We never had enough firewood but there was always plenty of furniture to burn – even if it meant sitting on the floor.

So sit back, pass out the glasses and make sure you have plenty of ice. Read one random page and pass it on. And remember, if you ever get bored or distracted, you can always burn the words and use them to keep warm.

Love Always,
-Markus Almond

PART ONE

THINGS TO SHOUT OUT LOUD AT PARTIES

He was standing on top of the church screaming, "I'm gonna jump." The rest of us were laughing and cheering, "Do it," raising our wine and tequila bottles in the air. We were all 50 feet in the sky dancing with strangers we had met only hours earlier at a bar – our feet gracefully stepping in time to a battery powered stereo on a tar-topped cathedral. Beneath our dancing feet, young lovers would wed in the spring and the elderly repented their sins every Sunday. We had our whole lives to find our brides and make our own sins. And the young man threatening us all with his own death settled by laughing hysterically and falling safely to his knees, then rolling over on his back to take a giant sip of red wine – spilling most of it onto his chin and neck.

Did human life come from fire and ice? An accidental combination of proteins and spinning energy? Is my consciousness the result of a trillion years of biological building blocks and unexplainable happenstance? I hope so. I feel like I could really kick some ass with that kind of luck on my side.

THINGS TO SHOUT OUT LOUD AT PARTIES

Let's shake our asses until the police kick us out. Let's go back in time and tell our younger selves that drugs aren't cool after all. Let's use our next paycheck to fill up the gas tank and head for the snowy crests of America's greatest.

To my surprise and smiling, tearing, eyes, I've found that this is by far the best time to be alive. We can have it all. Happiness and autonomy. Financial stability and free time. It's all right there if we perfect our skills and create something of value. The only thing left to do is take whatever it is that keeps you up at night and perfect it until it's an undeniable force.

THINGS TO SHOUT OUT LOUD AT PARTIES

You were too beautiful for words today. The neighbors looked and the firemen looked but you just stood on the sidewalk with your arching, high-heeled legs like a gazelle. And you carried the 12-pack of Stella without asking for help, because I had to take a phone call and honestly couldn't carry the beer and your beauty with one hand.

We woke up in the desert. I had a jacket across my chest and the staring wheel jammed into my elbow. She had a thin blanket laid over her while she slept on her side. The sun was coming up – purple and gold. I grabbed a plastic water bottle off the floor and splashed the morning onto my eyes. I could see my breath even with the windows up. I didn't wake her. I just started the car, blasted the heat and headed back for the highway. We would be out of Arizona by the time she woke for lunch.

THINGS TO SHOUT OUT LOUD AT PARTIES

Mind, miracle mind, do me no harm this time. And let all the stars align so that my hopes and dreams lay out in front of me and nothing lays behind but smiles and friends who will call again.

I don't know myself extraordinarily well but I can tell you a few things. I'm not interested in dress code requirements. I prefer a bowl of rice to a gourmet meal. I like my hair messed up and I don't mind feeling misplaced or looked at sideways.

THINGS TO SHOUT OUT LOUD AT PARTIES

I roll out of bed and can barely keep my knees level with the earth. Wash that awful taste out of my mouth and replace it with a nauseating mint. Start the water for tea. Play "Earnest Hemingway's Nobel Prize Acceptance Speech" on Spotify. Print whatever I wrote last night to see what my subconscious had to say. I begin to relive and prune the words so that they can grow stronger under the sober sun.

The beautiful girls – the ones who jump into the ocean with their clothes off and never drink more than their mothers would find appropriate. The ones who always insist on buying their own ticket even after you've told them that you'll put them on the guest list. Those bright-eyed beautiful girls are what makes the world spin I think. Without them the sun would just give up. They ask meaningful questions because they are sincerely interested and they don't feel like talking about themselves. But you don't care which one of you is speaking. It's a good night as long as you can gaze across the table at each other and the card at the bar hasn't been declined.

THINGS TO SHOUT OUT LOUD AT PARTIES

There will be plenty of time for sorrow tomorrow. Today we celebrate.

I met her in a rural town on tour and cancelled two shows because of her. 'Strep throat' we called it. But I fell in love hard. She took me to the river her family used to visit when she was a little girl. We swung from a rope and let go into the water. We took off our clothes and got mud on our feet.

THINGS TO SHOUT OUT LOUD AT PARTIES

Remember that time, that time you were drunk on red wine and forgot to look at the time and you wanted to play strip poker with Lucky Charm marshmallows instead of poker chips and you were ranting and raving about the new Alkaline Trio album and how I should really "give OK Go a chance" and your roommates came home and you told them a 30 minute story about your beta fish; then you smoked five cigarettes on the front porch and joked about how every time it flash floods outside you go swimming in the street but were worried about getting hepatitis C or some weird urinary tract infection? Well, I must have fallen in love with you that night because I haven't left your side or hit ignore on my cell phone ever since.

We turned those sheets into a work of art – pushing and twisting and bending them into a Picasso sculpture night after night. It would have been better to burn them afterwards. No detergent in the world can wash away passion of that magnitude.

THINGS TO SHOUT OUT LOUD AT PARTIES

I want to take my shoes off in freshly cut grass. I want to spray you with a garden hose. I want to climb a tree and have problems with washing the sap off my hands. I want to take you to the local flea market and have a good laugh about what people think is worth money. And I want to make dinner with you and sip wine under the stars. And I don't want to do this for a day or a long weekend. I want to do this for the rest of our lives and I want you to be there every night.

Advice to a young person: Never trust someone who claims to have all the answers. Pay your utility bills on time. If given a choice between a one-night-stand and a thoughtful discussion over coffee, always choose the one-night-stand and bring two condoms in case the first one breaks. Never talk too much and always de-tag yourself from unflattering Facebook photos.

THINGS TO SHOUT OUT LOUD AT PARTIES

The sexiest people I know have a kind heart and a very strong belief in themselves.

Don't let the bastards get you down, my friends. Take their powerless insults with a dignified smile. They may try to hurt you but it's only a sign of desperation. Stand clear of their destruction. Disassociate yourself from second-rate nonsense.

THINGS TO SHOUT OUT LOUD AT PARTIES

I'm trying to maintain. Avoiding airplanes. Declining meetings and social gathers in order to perfect something. Pouring my soul into every last bit of the thing. Tunnel vision, and I've been holding my breath for months. I make sacrifices in this world because I want to leave something behind.

Let's be honest here. Some days are wasted on casual conversation with dreamers and talkers and the only doer in the room keeps to himself – constantly looking at the time and smoking cigarettes until it's over. I have little patience for discussing things that will never be.

THINGS TO SHOUT OUT LOUD AT PARTIES

I still have all the photos and weird pieces of paper that we hung on our bedroom walls when we were living together in college. I don't have many belongings anymore but I still keep all of those tiny pieces of paper carefully preserved. They turn more yellow and brittle every year.

There are all kinds of things for writers to do if you're in New York. There are workshops for writers, and support groups for writers. There are yoga groups for writers and seminars for writers. Conferences and presentations, networking and publishing events with guest speakers. There are Meetups in bars hosted by girls named Moonbeam. There are a thousand ways to hand out business cards and feel good about yourself without getting any writing done at all.

THINGS TO SHOUT OUT LOUD AT PARTIES

This moment won't last long. I know it's easy to be focused on the future. But this moment is all there is. The opportunity for change may only be available today.

I'm not a religious man. But I can see things that tell me I'm connected with all and all is connected with me. And I love because it's my most natural state. And I remind myself to let go of anger as soon as I can remember to do that. And I believe I have a soul because I have smelled the first day of spring and I have listened to Aretha Franklin on vinyl. And the things I feel in those moments cannot be explained by science.

THINGS TO SHOUT OUT LOUD AT PARTIES

You are the center of gravity. You keep it together while others spin around you. This is the ultimate cool.

Here's a list of things to do to clear your head: befriend a stranger, start a band, pierce something, go out to a place you would have never gone to before, call someone you haven't talked to in years, start wearing dress clothes every day (or if you are required to already do this, start wearing grunge cardigans whenever possible), start a blog about something you know nothing about, get a weekend job at a coffee shop just to learn about lattes and talk to people. Don't over think it.

THINGS TO SHOUT OUT LOUD AT PARTIES

Sometimes, the best thing to do is to get the hell out of the house and shake things up a bit.

Whatever happened to having a drink and listening to records? Whatever happened to having a laugh or sitting in silence? Adults are so crazy the way they run around trying to prove things to each other. It's very embarrassing to them if they don't have something impressive to offer. They believe in resumes and twitter followers. They worship envy and climb ladders that lead to nowhere.

THINGS TO SHOUT OUT LOUD AT PARTIES

I feel like I could fly sometimes. Like the ceiling will open up like one of those giant football domes and my couch will hover right into the sky and blast into far away galaxies at full speed – my fingers dancing on the laptop keys, stopping for not even intergalactic sightseeing.

For those of you with cars, come pick me up! Let's go to a small ski town and drink rum until a couple of college-break sweeties invite us up for a dip in the hot tub.

PART TWO

THINGS TO SHOUT OUT LOUD AT PARTIES

I have a strong desire to shave my head and start walking west. The second day would be the hardest. My muscles would feel like they were hit by a truck. But the pain would slowly subside and I'd adapt to the walk just like anything else in life. Eventually, I'd arrive at the Pacific Ocean with bulging calves, clear lungs and a mangy head of hair. I'd have a good long dip in the cool crests of high water magic – reborn or at least forgiven.

Dancing in the parking lot with lights in her eyes – she shook all of her fears and worries away in the wind. We all looked on to figure out how she did it. Was it in her feet or the way she moved those knees of hers? Was it in that summer dress that she threw around like she was taunting a bull? Was it in that hair of hers that bounced and danced like a weeping willow in a rain storm? For a second we all thought she stole our fears and concerns and stomped them out cold with her own on the pavement. But when the dance stopped and she skipped off laughing ecstatic, those concerns came back to us on-lookers. We were ordinary and the power of dance was hers and hers alone.

THINGS TO SHOUT OUT LOUD AT PARTIES

Production value for music is a lot like clothes. You can wear popular clothes or homemade clothes, vintage clothes or expensive, designer clothes. But good songwriting and honest character will always trump fashion.

In junior high school, there were girls everywhere. They walked down the sunny halls and they were SO pretty. And I wanted to kiss them all. I wished that I was the only boy in Junior High so that all the girls paid more attention to me. And I didn't know what sex was but I knew it meant they would be naked and I wanted to do that with all of them.

THINGS TO SHOUT OUT LOUD AT PARTIES

To the girl who lives in Ohio: Our city is overcrowded and none of us like it when people move here. It raises the average cost of rent in our area and lessens the chance of finding a seat in our favorite bars. With that said, we've decided we can make an exception for you. You can thank the good people of Brooklyn.

They tell us we're only here for a short time. Then they tell us the most important thing is showing up to work on time and maxing out that 401K. But I don't know. Most nights I just wish we had a car and a couple bottles of wine to watch the sunrise from a city we've never been to before.

THINGS TO SHOUT OUT LOUD AT PARTIES

I'll never forget your spirit in 2006. I'll never take your name in vein even after your skin starts to sag and your tits look like the homeless woman that used to sleep outside our apartment when we lived in New York. I won't forget those windy laughs we had over the car stereo headed west in the Midwestern summer day light. When I call you on the phone (decades later) a wormhole opens up in the time-continuum and we are right back there in 2006 sipping on giant gas station sodas and smoking cigarettes through smiles, unsure and unconcerned whether we're in Montana or South Dakota.

We danced in studded belts and chains dangling intimidatingly from our wallets trying to kick our feet in the air as high as we could. And the lead singer SCREAMED into the microphone. Our fists swinging high, elbows out, heads nodding and trying to hide our smiles. The beer flowed for a dollar a can that night and we sweat out all our troubles in a wordless circle of bodies – distorted guitars all around us and I remember thinking, "So this is what family feels like." Those dirty fucking punks still make me smile.

THINGS TO SHOUT OUT LOUD AT PARTIES

This city is something else. Everyone's always running. They run faster and faster. Everyone is able to accomplish so much meaningless bullshit in a single day. It's a miracle our economy ever survived before the implementation of sole-padded dress shoes.

If I could have the temperament for anything I'd be a very successful and well-spoken investment banker. I'd wear expensive suits and I would sleep well at night. And I would have many children. But God or my ancestors or a random combination of neurotransmitters prohibits me from being driven by money. And between you and me, I would not have the patience to sit through a meeting about convertible bonds and interest rates.

THINGS TO SHOUT OUT LOUD AT PARTIES

I wish I could shoot fireworks out of my hands on command. I would go to night clubs in Manhattan and shine up the reflective foreheads of college beauties. I'd knock over cold bottles of Chrystal onto Wall Street business suits and tell the DJ to "STAND BACK" because I was about to bring explosions to the dance floor in a way that no one's ever seen before. And maybe I'd be the most loved firework dancer of all time or maybe they'd put me in jail with the other lunatics. But one thing's for sure, they better keep me away from the sprinklers or the pigs will be taking a shower for sure.

I remember we were prancing through New York months after the terrorists attacks buying rare editions of Iggy Pop albums on vinyl. We fell in love in Times Square not because we were infatuated but because we'd been falling for years and it kept us warm in the van. And I was like that glowing ball where every year people still wear those ridiculous glasses with the year on them. I can remember waking up with our coats on and scraping together enough coins to share an omelet in the morning. I couldn't help it then, or for the rest of my life, to be obsessed with your lioness eyes, tearing me to shreds with every blink.

THINGS TO SHOUT OUT LOUD AT PARTIES

If only I could get on that plane. That plane that always seems a bit too far out of my price range and never seems to be leaving at the time I need it too. If only I could just book my flight – the one that leads to white sands and crystal clear blue waves. There are stingrays under there but they never mean anyone any harm. They just want to live peaceful lives and not be bothered too much. If only I could stop struggling for a month and get out there to wish them, "Good day, stingray."

The man downstairs is always quite happy to see me. "Markus! Markus! What's new, Markus!?" I try to do the best I can do to make the words come. "Nice weather we're having today," I say. The poor old man lost his only son to diabetes last year. "My son worked from home too," the man said on fathers day. "I always told him he needed to exercise more," the man said on Easter. "Well, it's supposed to be nice weather all week," I tell him. "Goodbye, Markus!" he says. "Goodbye."

THINGS TO SHOUT OUT LOUD AT PARTIES

I sometimes see my great grandmother. In the afterlife she is six feet tall, has giant feathered wings and wears a thin white dress. I didn't realize it was her until I saw an old family picture recently. She was quite beautiful in her earthly youth and seems free and strong in the afterlife. She takes care of me when I need help.

I used to know this girl whose heart worked like a magnet – not the refrigerator kind but the kind that can pick up a car and lift it into the crusher. Now, I'm not saying that her intentions were to compress your bones and soul from all angles until there was nothing left but a lifeless cube. But I am saying that when her electromagnet heart was on full power, there was very little a man wouldn't do for her – even if his future was beginning to look more and more like scrap metal.

THINGS TO SHOUT OUT LOUD AT PARTIES

The most painful thing I can think of is loving someone who doesn't love you back. Wars must start this way.

Is it strange that I can taste music in my wine? I actually think of the taste in terms of audio waves. Like, "Oh, this wine has some really nice high frequencies but the low end isn't as strong as the '89 Merlot."

THINGS TO SHOUT OUT LOUD AT PARTIES

If free will does exist, then we must have made a wrong turn. Because we were supposed to be side-by-side fighting crime in this world with stolen paintings and drunken poetry – talking each other out of midnight morning guilt with the taste of stale cigarettes still on our tongues after young lovers left our beds in the early daylight. But somehow we were separated at birth and you're out there search searching for that muse in the moonlight and I'm out here trying to imagine what you're doing tonight and wondering if your girl for the evening is better looking than mine. Follow the stars my dear friend and we'll write the next chapter of this anthology with open hearts and open wounds – leaving the windows cracked to air them both out.

Jazz is the music of madmen. The melodies are all cut up like a heart surgery – the vital arteries sliced without remorse and pieced back together in a way that defies physics and God. I can actually SEE Picasso paintings when I listen to it, three or four separate angles of what the melody was supposed to sound like before it was dissected and scientifically destroyed by boredom and heroin.

THINGS TO SHOUT OUT LOUD AT PARTIES

I want to rent scuba diving equipment with you in countries we have never been to before. I want to rest my head on your breasts and order breakfast for you in the morning. I want to laugh with you at how bad we are at calculating exchange rates and worship your nipples with my tongue. I want to reminisce without ever looking back. I want to raise children without ever feeling old.

I quit smoking which led me to quit drinking - which was very difficult but led me to exercising quite often which lead me to going to sleep at a reasonable hour which lead me to not writing anymore. This lead me to nervousness and emptiness which lead me to drinking, and then to smoking and then to writing my ass off again and sleeping like a baby.

THINGS TO SHOUT OUT LOUD AT PARTIES

Ella was a ray of golden light. She danced and sang wherever she went, made breakfast in the mornings and called us both colorless and disheveled. I fell in love with her several times and always tried to talk myself out of it the next morning.

Growing old is a lot like learning how to take care of a car. When you first start driving it's really fun to speed and crash and take road trips and make love in the back seat. But when you get older you know you should really change the oil and keep an eye on the dashboard for engine warning lights. And it's still okay to fuck in the back but maybe put a blanket down so you don't mess up the resale value.

THINGS TO SHOUT OUT LOUD AT PARTIES

You saw me at a party and wanted to talk about something so I told you that one time I jumped off the Brooklyn bridge and swam all the way to the East Village and the first thing I did when I arrived was dry off under a hot-air hand dryer in a high-class restaurant. And you said the only hot-air blowing around were the words coming out of my mouth. And I asked you to have a drink with me but you said you didn't date liars or professional dancers. And I told you I'd give up dancing if you brushed your teeth before I took you to bed.

I cannot decipher the difference between your self-indulgent, hipster drug abuse and your truth-seeking enlightenment in the sunrise mornings of samsara. To me you all look like a bunch of fakers playing dress up – though I assume there is some wisdom hiding amongst you somewhere – even if it is a low percentage.

THINGS TO SHOUT OUT LOUD AT PARTIES

The heat is coming in strong waves in New York. The children outside unscrew the fire pump and dance in a strong arc of water – cooling everything and everyone within its reach. The air conditioner doesn't work very well on days like this and I have no choice but to type naked and to make as much ice as possible.

Well, there's that band that can fill a room with 3,000 people. They sell enough T-shirts on tour to buy a house (paying in sweaty stinking cash with a tour bus parked in back). And there's that writer who hides in a mansion somewhere outside Los Angeles. No one recognizes him but he can release journals from his high school years and still make the best seller list. He has movie options for books he hasn't even thought of yet. And then there's the rest of us wondering how to make that jump and barely keeping it together from paycheck to paycheck as our lovers grow tired and our family members stop calling.

She was beautiful. She wore more eye-makeup than KISS. Her clothes hung off of her like a romantic statue covered in silk for a 'made-for-TV' movie. God spent hours on each of her toes, making sure each was colored and fitted perfectly for such a walking piece of art. Those toes kept her well-balanced, even after I poured red wine in her blood stream and asked her to dance on wet dewy grass in McCarren Park.

Kristine isn't such a threat. She's a beautiful person really. And I don't think she means you any harm. If anything, she only wants to sweep up your broken pieces. She only wants to take them home and glue them back together in the garage.

I'm at Pete's Candy Shop listening to writers doing readings. Readings are terrible. I mean they WROTE it, couldn't they just remember it and act it out for us in real time. They are literally staring at the page like they had never seen the words before in their life. Even Bukowski was like that – stumbling over the rhythm he had put there himself, hiding behind a cheap cigar and staining the pages with red wine.

MARKUS ALMOND

I have no desire to speak in public.

THINGS TO SHOUT OUT LOUD AT PARTIES

Remember that time you took me to your family's lake house and I got so mad at you that I threw the oars from our row boat? We had no way of paddling. You just stared at me like I was insane. And I kept laughing. You were SO PISSED. And I didn't realize the paddles would float. I thought we'd be there for days. Days and days staring at the shore while suns and stars kept passing over us until we both forgot why we were angry.

Sometimes I get so terrified that I'm experiencing reality completely wrong. Like the way I see things is like a poodle in a world of Persian cats. Like my eyes and soul see and express things in a way that no other living life-form can ever relate to. And that's a lonely feeling. And it's a scary feeling and it's a self-doubtful feeling.

THINGS TO SHOUT OUT LOUD AT PARTIES

Ex-girlfriends are like smoking. Just because you want a cigarette doesn't mean they're any good for you.

MARKUS ALMOND

We had emotional guns pointed at each other's heads and smiled like they were lollipops.

THINGS TO SHOUT OUT LOUD AT PARTIES

You might feel melancholy while you try to hold on to all the people and memories that pass through your finger tips like an unfinished cigarette, stepped out on the pavement just as the Berlin train arrives. But there will be more nights and there will be fresh air to breathe and new memories to be made at the next stop – as long as you're quick-witted and eager enough to never miss your train.

Love is a library book that you must renew regularly.

THINGS TO SHOUT OUT LOUD AT PARTIES

I met the guys from Ash the other day. I've been listening to their song "Uncle Pat" for years. I really like that song. I meant to tell them this but instead just drank my wine and kept my thoughts to my goddamn self.

I am a loner. I rsvp to shit and never show up. My family doctor and I have never met. I once attended a Broadway show for a 'night out on the town' and left at intermission. The best time to catch me is during my late night walks in Central Park or in the morning when I'm too tired to remember that I don't enjoy answering the phone.

THINGS TO SHOUT OUT LOUD AT PARTIES

Writing a novel is like pushing a two ton boulder up a hill all by yourself. And just when you think you're done, someone hands you a chisel and a mallet and says, "Edit this until it looks like the statue of David."

There must be a way to shake ourselves awake without the use of drugs (heart attack, paranoia, earthquake). There must be a way to brush off the work day's grime and dust and open our eyes in time to find our free time, our me-time – the only time in our lives that we need to survive. Keep some love in your heart. Keep some energy in reserve. And when the time comes to create, let it pour out of you like a hurricane.

THINGS TO SHOUT OUT LOUD AT PARTIES

To the band who played at the Mercury Lounge last night: you should explore your options in custodial services and/or the educational programs at the community colleges in your area. Thank you.

What kings we were to sleep in a church for free, setting fires and taking the neighbors to bed. You just laid it all out there for us, didn't you, Lord? You gave us the world and we drank every last drop. And we refused to go into work the next day. We had no bills to pay and basked in the freedom of sleeping through hangovers and served each other breakfast on mismatched plates laid carefully on the floor.

THINGS TO SHOUT OUT LOUD AT PARTIES

The year I graduated college I made a list. A list of all that was important to me and everything I wanted to do before I died. I kept that list in my wallet for two years, and when I got a new wallet I placed it carefully in my sock drawer. And in between many different jobs and many different apartments and many different girlfriends and moving trucks, I lost that list along with half of my hooded sweatshirts and my collection of rare grunge LPs somewhere between Chicago and New York.

Let's run into that pet shop with shotguns and demand all of God's creatures be set free. Free the bulldog! Send the hamsters out into the streets. Central Park will be a wild place again. When the police aren't looking, we'll free their horses and spank 'em all a good one on the ass of freedom.

THINGS TO SHOUT OUT LOUD AT PARTIES

Let's dance on the rooftops that look over the Hudson. I'll buy the drinks if you promise to smile even after you've grown bored.

We drove the van as fast as the engine would let us. And we always invited people to come with us. We would bring along everyone we met if we could fit them in the van. We'd show up in Seattle or Portland and increase the population of unshowered punk rock girls – their makeup running and hair twisting into newly formed dreadlocks. Taking a vacation from society was always exhilarating and enlightening. But staying away for too long made coming back a jarring and difficult adjustment.

THINGS TO SHOUT OUT LOUD AT PARTIES

Sitting in the green room at Rockefeller Center, the make-up girls give me the stink eye because I declined stage make-up just like that last time I was here. The biggest problem with these late shows is that you have to take the elevator six floors down just to have a cigarette, and the only time the host is funny is when he trips on his way out.

I miss playing in a band. I miss guitar tuners and PA systems and the back seats of vans. I miss trying to sell T-shirts, eating bad food and trying desperately to find a condom.

THINGS TO SHOUT OUT LOUD AT PARTIES

In San Francisco in 2001, you could smell the ocean in the air somewhere between the Mission district and the Tenderloin. In the daylight I would walk for hours stopping to watch skateboarders or to take in the energy of an anti-war rally. My thoughts were on the car accident I had experienced that morning and whether or not I'd have a place to sleep that night.

Sometimes I feel like I've split my ribcage and taken out my soul and given it to you. But you seem nice enough.

THINGS TO SHOUT OUT LOUD AT PARTIES

I miss the way she would enter a room after a fresh shower – eyes still batting tap water and skin steaming and goose bumped. I miss the way she would tell me everything was fine even during my darkest moments.

She had never seen a sex swing before and I had to teach her how to use it. "It's very simple," I explained. "You just sit here like this and make sure your butt is on this part." Four hours later we both passed out from physical exhaustion.

THINGS TO SHOUT OUT LOUD AT PARTIES

America the beautiful, I worry you've given up on producing physical products and our economy is built on a service-era, data-building, Ponzi scheme. I worry I should be hiding my cash in the mattress and backing up all my blog posts in hand written scribbles. I think one day we'll have nothing but wires and screens. If a comet hits, no one will know about us. When the internet is demolished, there will be no record of our culture and insight. I hope our descendants can recover the Instagram servers.

Shooting guns in an old house without air conditioning. The same old song has been on repeat since 2am. Our neighbors are all asleep or too drunk to roll over and call the police. The women have all left and we're all too drunk for actual conversation. We spar in the living room and break lawn chairs in the front yard – setting fire to anything made of wood and forgetting that under all our yells and blank-eyed laughter are actual human beings with breathing mothers and siblings. They'd shake their heads in disapproval if they knew just how far we had truly fallen.

THINGS TO SHOUT OUT LOUD AT PARTIES

I could see my own reflection in the waxed tiles and I looked like a walking dead person or at least someone released from the hospital a week or two earlier than they should have been.

Six times I saw her without saying anything. Six times I tried not to notice her beauty and the way she held her iPhone sideways when she texted. Six times she filled my peripheral vision like fireworks as I pretended not to notice her. She tortured me with that beauty on six separate occasions. When I saw her for the seventh time, we made love on my porch and I proposed marriage first thing in the morning.

The thunder storm swallowed up the moonlight and turned our town into a black hole of pouring rain. We came across a lake and dared each other to dive in. The water was so deep our toes wouldn't reach the bottom. It sent a wave a fear through me at first because I couldn't see her. I couldn't see anything but rain and lightning every few seconds. I had to call out that angel's name and we swam toward each other. Finally, I got her close enough to reach out and pull her toward me in that black lake abyss. I held her body against mine as the rain pounded into the lake water. She was smiling and shivering and I kissed her. A bolt of God's white lightning crashed in the water and she let out a nervous laugh - a beautiful laugh. There was so much rain we weren't even sure where the lake ended and the storm began. We pressed our bodies up against each other and kept kicking. I wiped the cold, wet, curls out of her eyes and kissed her like we were flying in space.

PART THREE

THINGS TO SHOUT OUT LOUD AT PARTIES

You don't get many second chances in this world. Don't turn your back on them. You don't get many true loves. Embrace the ones in your life and set your fears aside. You only get two parents. Forgive them. Not every business in this country will willingly hand you a paycheck. Do your work with presence. And if the stars align and the heavens deem your art acceptable enough for an audience, love every new friend and never put ads on your website.

She had legs like a battle, kicking and shooting into the air in all directions – healthy and tan, firm and toned, smooth and sexy. She bounced when she laughed in bed. We had a cheap box spring and I wouldn't have it any other way. I felt her giggle all over my sides and toes as the springs beneath us bounced in a happy dance. Tempur-Pedic would have been isolating torture.

THINGS TO SHOUT OUT LOUD AT PARTIES

We shared a shower and I mowed her lawn for her.

I sit on this very short stretch of time. I'll soon be gone and everything I do will eventually be washed away. So I would like you to know that I'm thinking of you today – and every day – that we might spend these blinking moments together and pass on to whatever's next – both waiting for the other.

THINGS TO SHOUT OUT LOUD AT PARTIES

Befriend someone who loves your personality and not your social status. They will be there for you when the stock market collapses.

I will still love you when you're fat and old and your beauty is hidden to the casual observer, deep in the center of your eyes, in your memories of youth and finding love for the first time. It's my life's privilege to have been with you while you were a teenager and by your side for every year watching your hair turn grey and your smile grow even more beautiful each morning. I hope there is a heaven. Because I don't think I could handle emptiness without you.

THINGS TO SHOUT OUT LOUD AT PARTIES

Young people, break all the hearts you can while you're still clean and thin. Put your bodies to good work while you're still invincible.

If you don't feel like a blooming flower when you're with your friends, you've got to let them go. We're here to prop each other up and help each other out. If you can't lean on your buddies like a wine grape vine on a chain link fence, you need to spread you're roots until you find solid ground.

THINGS TO SHOUT OUT LOUD AT PARTIES

Dave put on a dress during the party and the neighbor girl stuck mascara on his eyes. He was as straight as a football coach on the International Date Line. But that night he had too much to drink and thought it'd be a good idea to put on a discarded dress and dance like a New York Doll. A girl I was seeing came over and said, "Who the fuck is that?" I said, "That's Dave, my roommate." She said, "Why is he wearing my dress?" I said, "That's your dress?" She said, "Yeah, I left it here. I left my underwear too." It took a few more songs and three more tequila shots but we all learned that Dave was wearing those underwear too.

I wish society was set up in a way were it was okay to dance on the top of newspaper machines in the rain. I wish my friends wouldn't look at me strange when I bring my own vodka bottle to the bar and demand that the waitress play spin the bottle with us. I wish it was a-okay to do spontaneous jigs at car washes, funerals, sporting events, poetry readings, garage sales, dog parks, movie theatres, first dates, last dates, divorce attorney meetings and alcoholics anonymous. I sure wish we could all wear top hats and tip them to every pretty lady on Bedford Ave. And I don't mean tip our hats in a rushed sort of a way, I mean take the whole thing off, bow down and flip it over like they used to do in the movies.

THINGS TO SHOUT OUT LOUD AT PARTIES

Her dress twisted and spun like a mangled roll of paper towels – flowers and strips of material floated in all directions like confetti. She was a malting bird of beauty, that one. She dragged me around to bars and parties all over the city and left a trail of feathers and beaded necklaces behind her. I told her that if we got too high, we could use her dress as a parachute.

I don't know this and I can never know for sure, but when we were in college, or more accurately, when you were in college and I was drinking full-time, I have a sneaking suspicion that you put a tiny dab of perfume just above your vagina before you came to bed each night. And like I said, too many years have passed and I can never know for sure, but if I were in Las Vegas and there were a table where people bet on such things, I'd put all my money on you and that smell that used to drive me wild.

THINGS TO SHOUT OUT LOUD AT PARTIES

I called her on the old rotary phone the one where if you're had a lot of 9's or 0's in your number, it would take a good three minutes to dial. But eventually she answered and I picked her up wearing nothing but jean shorts and a smile and I lost those jean shorts somewhere on the beach and we were both walking funny by the time I dropped her off again.

You look beautiful tonight. When I hold your hand I can see the future – little babies crawling around with your eyes and my fucked up skin – phone calls always going to the answering machine because we can never get to them on time. The days come and go with the sun setting on little heads and adult smiles but that's years away. For now I just wanted to say, "Damn, girl. You look nice."

THINGS TO SHOUT OUT LOUD AT PARTIES

I always feel such sadness when I see a beautifully designed advertisement. I feel sad because I know this is a person with real talent who for some reason came to the conclusion that the only thing for them to do was to sell perfume and plus-sized skirts at Macy's. The layout is beautiful and the content cowardly.

We exercised for the sole reason of being better lovers at night. We stretched our stamina for one reason alone – so that we could experience each other's bodies together and push them to limits no level-headed person had ever been to before.

THINGS TO SHOUT OUT LOUD AT PARTIES

You've got to do what makes you happy. And I don't mean fly to Vegas and shack up with an over-paid and under-weight hooker doing Jägerbombs until you're both too drunk too see. I mean giving serious thought to choosing what will result in year-to-year happiness.

If we don't have art we don't have much. If we have hours of work we don't enjoy, the bums on the street are richer than us. If we don't have an outlet to create and show our souls with welded metal or midnight blog posts, we're turning our backs on whatever nameless power put us here. If we're not making hard choices to accept life over money, we could learn a thing or two from our children.

THINGS TO SHOUT OUT LOUD AT PARTIES

Leaping off a cliff with a beer in my hand, I land safely in the ocean blue with nothing left to do but float and let go.

I am pretty insignificant in the general perspective of things.

THINGS TO SHOUT OUT LOUD AT PARTIES

Growing old is a painful and humiliating thing if you follow the rules of 9 to 5 and twice-a-year vacations. But old age can be a strong and beautiful privilege if you find a groove that gets you jumping out of bed every morning. The smile-line wrinkles cut a deep badge of happiness if you remember to chase the joy before it's gone.

He swore he could hold his breath longer than anyone. "Let's make it interesting," I said holding up a roll of duck tape. Everyone at the party was very upset when we had to call the paramedics.

THINGS TO SHOUT OUT LOUD AT PARTIES

There was this night in Japan when we got drunk on piss-warm beer and came home and giggled with our hands over our mouths. The locals chowed down on raw eggs and raw ground beef. I danced nude on the coffee table and gave strong lectures about E. coli and salmonella.

I think escalators are a good way to ensure our grandchildren have the fattest asses the world has ever seen.

THINGS TO SHOUT OUT LOUD AT PARTIES

I enjoy writing in bed and fucking in bed and I sometimes even enjoy dreaming in bed. My favorite part about leaving the house and seeing the sparkling world is knowing that I can return home when I choose too and I can snuggle with the girl I love under carefully purchased comforters with the word 'comfort' built into them before we even fell in love in the first place.

Sometimes I feel like I can jump off rooftops and fall in love a thousand times and never get my heart broken. Psychologists call this state mania, but I don't know, I think maybe it's a connection to love and spirituality. Because what happens when your body really dies? Sure they put the remains in a casket but something tells me there's much more happening with the soul after it leaves the body. Something we can only feel and never explain. Something much more beautiful than writing poems on your cellphone while waiting for the goddamn G train to show up.

THINGS TO SHOUT OUT LOUD AT PARTIES

My biggest enemy is myself. He's a relentless prick sometimes. I have to keep reminding him that I'm in charge here and we have important things to do.

To My Ex-Lover: I just wanted you to know that I ran into a couple of our old friends and they've become fat and miserable. Remember those friends whose tits we held like a fresh fruit that God himself had created. You were experimenting with girls and I was experimenting with being arrogant. Those may have been the best days of our youth. And it looks like after all those years, the fresh fruits have fallen and those young peaches have given birth to future college girls – eager to explore their own sexualities. Please do not respond. I do not wish to encounter a recent photo of you on the internet. The ones I have from 10 years ago will suit me just fine.

THINGS TO SHOUT OUT LOUD AT PARTIES

Honor your soul. You'll be dead before you know it. You may be dead tomorrow for all I know. Do you really want to waste your time on earth? You've got a great opportunity ahead of you. I don't know what it is. Only you can know that for sure. Don't doubt yourself. Don't be afraid. Be smart and run for it like a skydiver chases adrenaline.

He was a strange guy. He played the flute on the weekends and shot heroine afterwork on Thursdays. He had a job down at the food processing plant on the outskirts of town. I guess his drug guy worked there and they had the same shift on Thursday. I always had to check to make sure he didn't have any cigarettes going before I went to sleep.

THINGS TO SHOUT OUT LOUD AT PARTIES

Sometimes there's nothing worse than being predictable.

You were the actress too stupid or weird to listen to all your classmate's advice. They graduated with a passion for acting but sought out husbands, children and a happy, predictable life. You were far too weird for all of that. You chose to make your own path and grew to be nothing short of extraordinary. Your old classmates still see you sometimes in the movies or on televised award shows. Every year they talk about what a strange girl you were, and how you never listened to their advice.

THINGS TO SHOUT OUT LOUD AT PARTIES

I'm not sure I agree with all these shiny buildings and designer clothes. I'm not sure I follow the creed of 60 hour work weeks and I don't think all of the women here are as beautiful as all the tourists say they are. Yes, they look lovely, soft and clean under a bright light but give them a moral compass and they're as lost as a fish in space.

In this life, when you're standing on top of a 4-floor apartment complex, waving your underwear on a burning stake and screaming, "The stars are temporary and so are we," your neighbors refuse to admit your significance in the world. They call the police and the landlord stuffs your mail box with eviction notices. But after you're long gone, those old couples toss in the sheets and realize that even with the silence, they still have trouble sleeping.

THINGS TO SHOUT OUT LOUD AT PARTIES

Some of us drink too much. Some of us fuck too much. Some of us love clothes so much we buy jeans too much. But we try our bests and we help each other out. We have all loved and lost and we try to keep afloat in this fast-paced world. We have broken hearts but we get up in the morning anyway.

There will be perfection in your smile even while you sleep. And there will be beauty in your eyes even while they're closed. And I'll have love in my heart while I'm gone or even deceased. Because I know that you are my world even after I've left it. I think I might meet you half-way in Pennsylvania or purgatory. I'll keep the bed warm. And if I never come back to you in the physical form, at least I know that we've become entangled and will always be connected no matter where I go.

THINGS TO SHOUT OUT LOUD AT PARTIES

Two O'clock in the morning I'm smoking a cigarette in a Hurricane. I've heard the power went out in Queens hours ago when the rain was only falling at a slight angle. Now the glowing streams are dropping at 45 degrees and will soon be completely horizontal. I am holding an umbrella for the sole reason of keeping my cigarette lit. Otherwise, I would stand in the street naked and careless at the thought of wind or rain washing me away. The neighborhood starts to flood around me. God attempts to threaten or shake my nerves with a flash of lightning. But the only result is a quick view of the streets – my retinas reflect with indifference and a slight disdain.

I loved her. I loved her with everything I had. And I broke her. By the end, we were both stumbling around in a daze, couldn't even form sentences. Had to leave her. Had to save us both by leaving her. Still regret it but know there was no other way to save her.

THINGS TO SHOUT OUT LOUD AT PARTIES

The void is the place you're afraid to look at. It's the unknown, the blankness where nothing you know is true and everything you imagined is possible. You're fears are there. They're ready to manifest and make your life a living hell. But bliss is down there too if you're brave enough to find it. The void is endless possibilities and infinite dimensions all rolled up into a reaction. It's waiting to see what you bring to the table. Choose to see goodness and the void will never let you down.

He drove himself crazy with phone calls unanswered and designated meeting places left stood up. He loved her but didn't know it yet. He thought it was all great fun, this girl that popped into his skull every morning the moment he woke up. Time and time again, there she was – her smile, the sound of her voice. "She's super hot but I don't want anything serious," he said. He didn't realize he was in love until she stopped showing up. He didn't know how much he longed for her until he was alone in a car sobbing at the thought of never seeing her again.

THINGS TO SHOUT OUT LOUD AT PARTIES

I've always been a terrible salesman. I used to get really worried about it. "Everyone's selling something," the successful people said. "Whether you're selling yourself at a job interview or selling your personal brand to a client." They even said, "Maybe you're selling an idea to your husband that he needs to take out the trash." It took me a long time to figure out what they meant by that. And then one day, I finally figured it out: salesmen are fucking assholes.

Ella was afraid of all of us. She always spoke very loudly and never jumped in without leaving one foot firmly planted in her past. She had loved and lost and tried to force herself to get over it. But she was just like the rest of us – damaged and scared shitless of having her heart broken again.

THINGS TO SHOUT OUT LOUD AT PARTIES

These waves of depression come when you least expect it. One minute you're living in heaven and ready to take over the world, the next you're ready to die – anything to set the soul free from this ugly and starving perspective. You know it isn't right but it's the only point of view you've got.

She reflected the stars and moon off of her like a midnight roller coaster. Drips of dew clung to her because she was the coolest thing moving in the summer air. Her smile lit the highways for truckers and businessmen to find their way home. And although you can't capture the sky, I'll be damned if I didn't try. And she was mine for a while – a short while but the best I've known.

THINGS TO SHOUT OUT LOUD AT PARTIES

Do you ever feel like you're losing it? Like your view of the world is completely wrong and everybody in the room is upside down but you? Like the voice coming out of your throat isn't even yours and the words it's saying aren't even what you believe? Maybe those people don't know how to see you for you. Maybe you should roll with somebody as beautiful as you are.

Girl, sometimes the earth is upside down and my feet are in space and I can't stand up straight because there's nothing to put my feet on out there. And it's cold and everyone looks at me weird because I'm upside down and keep slipping without you.

THINGS TO SHOUT OUT LOUD AT PARTIES

How do we turn it off? How do we take a break? When does the vacation start? How do we calm down? Why do I feel like I'm going to be sick? Carnival ride sick. Yelling at the conductor to "please turn it off" sick.

PART FOUR

THINGS TO SHOUT OUT LOUD AT PARTIES

In another life I would have called her my muse – receiving my 3am phone calls, laughing at my desperate derangement, humoring ideas that were limited in nature and caused by a temporary cloud of chemical induced insanity. But when the sun comes up, the smoke clears and I stumble out of bed, she's still in the writing, between the lines – for better or worse.

Maybe bravery doesn't mean pretending to be strong but instead means having the courage to admit when we are weak – so that even in our most vulnerable moments, we are self-assured enough to lean back and let the universe carry us to stable ground again.

THINGS TO SHOUT OUT LOUD AT PARTIES

I'm from a time when people danced to rock bands in bars full of smoke, when friends talked on real telephones plugged into walls for hours on end, when pictures came in white paper envelopes from the corner store and the internet was just a passing craze.

I knew a girl once who saw my soul and loved every part of it. I left her somewhere in Boston or Detroit. I thought nothing of it at the time but the joke was on me. My soul had crawled up inside her and I've been half a man ever since that muggy day in August.

She had these little workout socks that stuck up just above her running shoes. And from there it was all leg – leg from the floor to her tiny mesh gym shorts. I wanted to take a ride on those legs and see how they spent the day – stretching and firming themselves, sweating in the warmth of the sun before the final hot shower of the day.

I'm confused about the part of life where everyone goes out all the time and has sex with each other and dances until 4am and then the part where everyone picks a life partner and tries to have children, gets real jobs and never goes out again. It seems like an unreasonable transition.

THINGS TO SHOUT OUT LOUD AT PARTIES

I'm really not interested in aging.

If we sell everything we own, we would have just enough for a sail boat and a tank of gas to get us out into the open ocean. From there we'll ride the storm to freedom.

THINGS TO SHOUT OUT LOUD AT PARTIES

She left town and what do you do when part of your soul leaves town. Most people just ignore it. Others have a good cry and make an honest attempt to get better. And a very select few, the weird ones, try to re-create that missing piece with drugs and music and mindless sex and throwing everything else away.

Some days I feel like I'm as lost as the sand.

THINGS TO SHOUT OUT LOUD AT PARTIES

I am older now and I am more mature. One might even say that I am more happy. But I still miss some things about the old days. I miss waking up without a hangover and I miss smoking cigarettes with girls I'd never met before. I miss naked strangers and learning new chords on the guitar. I miss quitting jobs without ever second guessing myself or losing faith in the future. I miss strong drink, empty bank accounts and young laughter. I miss being around people as crazy as I used to be. We were never embarrassed to strip nude at a house party.

Kurt I miss the way your eyes cut through press interviews and your voice was the only thing on the radio worth believing in. I'm sorry your face is now forever on the bedroom walls of stoners and your association with Hendrix and Janis Joplin can never be broken. You were the punk rock Jesus to those paying attention and you changed some minds for the better.

THINGS TO SHOUT OUT LOUD AT PARTIES

We spent our entire paychecks at the porn store that week. She bought edible lotions, a dog collar, spreadable chocolate and raspberry pastes that could be eaten off any body part, one cock ring, four leather straps and two boxes of flavored condoms. She called in sick to work for three days. I paid for the room in advance and brought no change of clothes.

I wish I would have read a couple of sales books before I met you. I wish I had a masters degree in persuasion so I could tell you all of the reasons why you shouldn't leave.

THINGS TO SHOUT OUT LOUD AT PARTIES

The snow started falling in October that year. Not even all the leaves had come undone yet, but there it was, small white flakes of ice, floating down into the grass and melting when it touched the sidewalks. We were all looking forward to Halloween. Young Patti was going to be a pregnant ballerina and Lou was planning on being a lonely angel.

There was a time when you and I were a couple of firecrackers. We were going to be together forever and make the rest of the universe jealous. We had lightning in a bottle and cut our hands on the glass before we could even find the cap.

THINGS TO SHOUT OUT LOUD AT PARTIES

Sometimes the people we love the most aren't equipped to love us back the way we wish they could. It doesn't mean we should love them any less.

Halloween in Brooklyn – I saw Kurt Cobain tonight. He looked good – like he didn't even realize he was dead. And his band played an eight song set at 285 Kent. They played Teen Spirit for their encore and he looked just as bored and desperate as the day his right tennis shoe appeared in the papers.

Dear Mr. God, sometimes I don't understand why you put people in our lives and then take them away. I understand and respect death. But I'm talking about the people who are still alive. They're out there right now. And somewhere deep down, they're the same people they used to be. But best friends become strangers and ex-lovers marry people we've never heard of. I don't understand why this happens, Mr. God. Maybe you could make the world a little bit smaller? Maybe you could make us like an African tribe where everyone takes care of each other and no one wanders.

I tried to say something useful and no words came. I tried to make a difference or spark excitement but no words came. I even tried to be original. And the only thought I had was that I had no thoughts at all. And that to me, had to be okay. Because I knew that if I fought that feeling of being lost, if I fought the confusion, it would suck me up like quicksand.

THINGS TO SHOUT OUT LOUD AT PARTIES

I have loved and lost and torn myself up at night attempting to let it go – dedicating years of my life to meditation and Buddhist philosophies in an attempt to forget you. But still you come to me in half-awake visions and whiffs of perfume from strangers on the subway. Decades will pass without your laugh or morning smile ever fading from my bruised and gratefully indebted amygdala.

I need some sort of house under the stars where there's no one to judge me or interrupt my sleep in the morning.

THINGS TO SHOUT OUT LOUD AT PARTIES

People have to be inherently good. Don't they? Once our basic needs are taken care of, don't we switch mindsets from primitive animals to unbreakable links in the chain of community? I just can't believe that people don't have each other's backs. I don't want to view the world that way.

She sat on the back of her parent's porch with me, hugging me sideways. She was more emotional than me when I told her I was going to quit the band. "When are you going to tell them?" she asked almost with tears in her eyes. I had been talking about it for months and it was on that porch that I realized I should have felt something – remorse, sadness, an intense longing for the past maybe, but all I felt was a cool damp breeze from a storm that passed hours ago and the wet grass under my feet.

THINGS TO SHOUT OUT LOUD AT PARTIES

I type in the dark with sunglasses on. The computer brightness is turned down all the way. If it were up to me, the monitor would be off and I'd just wake up in the morning and sort out the sentences, delete the nonsense and publish what still seems true in the daylight – editing out the word 'fuck' whenever possible.

You can thank me by leaving bottles of wine outside my door and never knocking.

THINGS TO SHOUT OUT LOUD AT PARTIES

The problem with Phil was that you never knew if you were talking to him or to the 12 beers he had just drank. He was happy and easy to adore when he was laughing and playing with the toddlers, but he also played a little rougher than you were comfortable with. And though you loved him and his rough hands he had lived a hard life by choice and there was always a little bit of "crazy" in his eyes – jumping off European mountains on hang gliders and stealing San Francisco street cars in the early days of his youth.

MARKUS ALMOND

After a long night of being charming, I prefer at least seven days of solitude and paranoia.

THINGS TO SHOUT OUT LOUD AT PARTIES

Due to the ongoing bedbug problem in New York, I cannot attend your show on Saturday. I will however gladly stand outside the theatre and spray people with RAID as they enter.

She was an old and prideful woman – divorced before divorce was in vogue. She would never remarry. Her first husband was enough tragedy for one life, she decided sometime ago. Her life didn't appear to have much in it other than working at the grocery store and cooking dinner in the evenings. She even volunteered to pick up weekend shifts for the extra money. But if you looked at her or talked with her, you couldn't help but think she had some sort of secret that was keeping it all together. She never talked about God or went to church but there was something in her eye – maybe the pride of living on her own without having to depend on a drunken and wildly abusive husband to pay the rent.

THINGS TO SHOUT OUT LOUD AT PARTIES

One of the guys in the band yesterday asked me if I would watch his guitar for him since I was outside anyway. They were so nice. They thanked me for coming and told me how excited they were to be playing in Williamsburg. I had no problem watching their stuff for them while they went inside to get more drinks. It's so nice meeting new people. In an unrelated note, I'm currently selling a green Fender Jaguar guitar (case included) and two Fender reverb amplifiers so please email if you're interested. I'm also selling a Chevy 8-passenger van.

I am not the son you took to the beach, yelling from the shore, "Don't go out too far." I have been around the world with young maidens, snorting God's white earth through plastic straws and one dollar bills. I have won and lost love and tossed careers into the wind for peace in my heart. I've sung a thousand songs written by my own heart and hands. I've tangoed in Berlin and vomited in Rome. You may still see that pale skinned, blue eyed boy smiling at the skies with orange hair in his eyes – but those bones grew strong and then fell frail again. This small boy swam until all land disappeared and the tides were far too strong to ever bring him back.

THINGS TO SHOUT OUT LOUD AT PARTIES

The thing I've never liked about life is that all my favorite moments are gone before I even know they're my favorite and the ones I love all move away or die before I get the chance to give a real goodbye.

The key to success is running towards what you're scared of – that and being so full of shit that you have no plan B.

THINGS TO SHOUT OUT LOUD AT PARTIES

There was a time when I really thought I'd live forever. I used to think I could do anything, you know. I thought I could be a singer in a band or a big time CEO. And I thought I could buy a thousand acres of land or travel the world indefinitely. I thought I'd be able to drink gallons of tequila and never get a hangover. I thought I could love with all my heart and never get hurt. And I thought everyone I knew would live forever.

Good-bye mom. Your hair still flows in 1985. The most beautiful smile a 4-year-old had ever seen. I'm sorry I turned into a man and you were left with no bundle of joy to hold. You were quite the catch before I was around, walking barefoot in condos you and dad couldn't afford. But there were nights when your sons let you forget the stack of bills on the counter and the empty refrigerator. And before you newly married lovers had tense discussions about financial plans, and before a tear hit your pillow as you drifted off to sleep, I made you smile as I learned new phrases and how to use a fork at the dinner table.

THINGS TO SHOUT OUT LOUD AT PARTIES

Some days I just want to throw it all up in a big explosion of flames and deleted emails. Sometimes I want all the voice mail messages to just rot there. Some nights I want to change my name and leave town immediately.

I woke up without my jacket by the river in the freezing cold, laying in snow. My iPhone had a crack across it and wouldn't light up. There weren't any footprints around me. I must have been out for most of the night. Where do these mornings come from and how to I get back to the warmth of my apartment?

THINGS TO SHOUT OUT LOUD AT PARTIES

I cut my self on a potato peeler while juicing vegetables. I was bleeding all over the counter and the sink. At that point it was decided to bandage the thing as best as I could and to go back to bed.

Writing felt good. It kept my demons at bay – the noise of the world was drowned out with sweet music that only I could hear. I didn't know if the electricity would be turned off on Tuesday or Wednesday but I had candles out and the manual typewriter next to my laptop just in case.

THINGS TO SHOUT OUT LOUD AT PARTIES

I do what I can to combat mortality and the smallness of the world. I would fall to my demise without the bodies of friends to lean on during the 3am walk home.

I think it might be storming outside but I haven't been in clean air in days. The window was boarded up long ago, for temperature reasons, and I've just been too hung up on typing to check the mail or go out for more coffee beans. Even the alcohol was last sipped up days ago. I'm low on cigarettes though, so it's only a matter of hours before I find out if my T-shirt will suffice in the possible storm that seems to be thundering through the walls and ceiling.

THINGS TO SHOUT OUT LOUD AT PARTIES

So when you meet the great maker – or so they say – tell him I'd like my money back and my youth back, and tell him I'd like a girl as crazy as I was – crashing newly purchased four-doors into reputable university buildings and howling like a madman, still naked and shivering from the cold when the police cars arrive.

Well, I'm not sure what else to say. I think of you every day though I'm expected not to and I've written more words for you than the common man would expect or accept and I've kept this all to myself – baring a secretive cross heavier than a subway train I take to places that remind me of 'us.' These places haunt the quiet pauses in casual conversations with people who have no idea about you – people who have never sat in the same room as your beauty. And I nod and smile, sip my drink and wonder what day this weight I carry will disappear and if it came all at once or was slowly accumulated over midnight madness, sexcipades and morning arguments leading up to the final good-bye.

CONCLUSION

Thank you for reading Things To Shout Out Loud At Parties. I really appreciate you taking the time to read it. If you care to read more of my stuff, including my upcoming novel, please sign up for my email newsletter at MarkusAlmond.com.

I would like to thank everyone who gave my last book a 5-star review on Amazon. Thank you Amanda, Robert C. Amann, Holly B., Brandon J. Campell, Nicole Coyle, Patti Edmon, Amanda Eldridge, Justin W. Foust, George Glass, Jacqueline Hang, Kelsey Ives, Walter B. Martens, Brandon Monk, David Paull, Nadia Payan, Matthew Pickle, Joseph Ratliff, The Rosskonian, Sal, Rosco Spears, Russell Wilson, Justin Woods and all you other awesome people. I hope one day we can all have a giant party together.

Thank you for everything.
-Markus Almond

If you enjoyed this book you may also like:

This book will break a window if you throw it hard enough.

Available Now.

ABOUT THE AUTHOR

Markus Almond is a punk rocker. He spent many years touring and writing music as the lead singer in a punk band. He once played CBGBs in his underwear. You can sometimes still hear his songs on MTV. Markus Almond currently lives in New York City where he now writes books, manages a record label and publishes a magazine.

Printed in Poland
by Amazon Fulfillment
Poland Sp. z o.o., Wrocław